DISCARD

CLINTON PUBLIC LIBRARY
306 8th Ave. S
Clinton, Iowa 52732

33691003346142

Help the Polar Bears

by Grace Hansen

Abdo Kids Jumbo is an Imprint of Abdo Kids
abdobooks.com

10/19

abdobooks.com

Published by Abdo Kids, a division of ABDO, P.O. Box 398166, Minneapolis, Minnesota 55439.
Copyright © 2019 by Abdo Consulting Group, Inc. International copyrights reserved in all countries.
No part of this book may be reproduced in any form without written permission from the publisher.
Abdo Kids Jumbo™ is a trademark and logo of Abdo Kids.
102018

012019

THIS BOOK CONTAINS
RECYCLED MATERIALS

Photo Credits: iStock, Shutterstock

Production Contributors: Teddy Borth, Jennie Forsberg, Grace Hansen

Design Contributors: Dorothy Toth, Laura Mitchell

Library of Congress Control Number: 2018946055

Publisher's Cataloging-in-Publication Data

Names: Hansen, Grace, author.

Title: Help the polar bears / by Grace Hansen.

Description: Minneapolis, Minnesota : Abdo Kids, 2019 | Series: Little activists: endangered species | Includes glossary, index and online resources (page 24).

Identifiers: ISBN 9781532182037 (lib. bdg.) | ISBN 9781532183010 (ebook) | ISBN 9781532183508 (Read-to-me ebook)

Subjects: LCSH: Polar bear--Juvenile literature. | Wildlife recovery--Juvenile literature. | Endangered species--Juvenile literature. | Ice--Arctic regions--Juvenile literature.

Classification: DDC 333.954--dc23

Table of Contents

Polar Bears

Polar bears roam the coldest places on Earth. They live in the Arctic.

The Arctic is the northernmost area on Earth. Arctic seas have sea ice. This is where polar bears hunt their favorite food, seals!

Status

Polar bears are considered **vulnerable**. This means that they may become **endangered**. Especially if threats to them do not stop.

Polar bears face several threats. The Arctic is far away from most people. But it is not safe from **pollution**.

Wind and ocean currents bring **chemicals** to parts of the arctic. Seals absorb these chemicals. Polar bears then take in the chemicals when they eat seals.

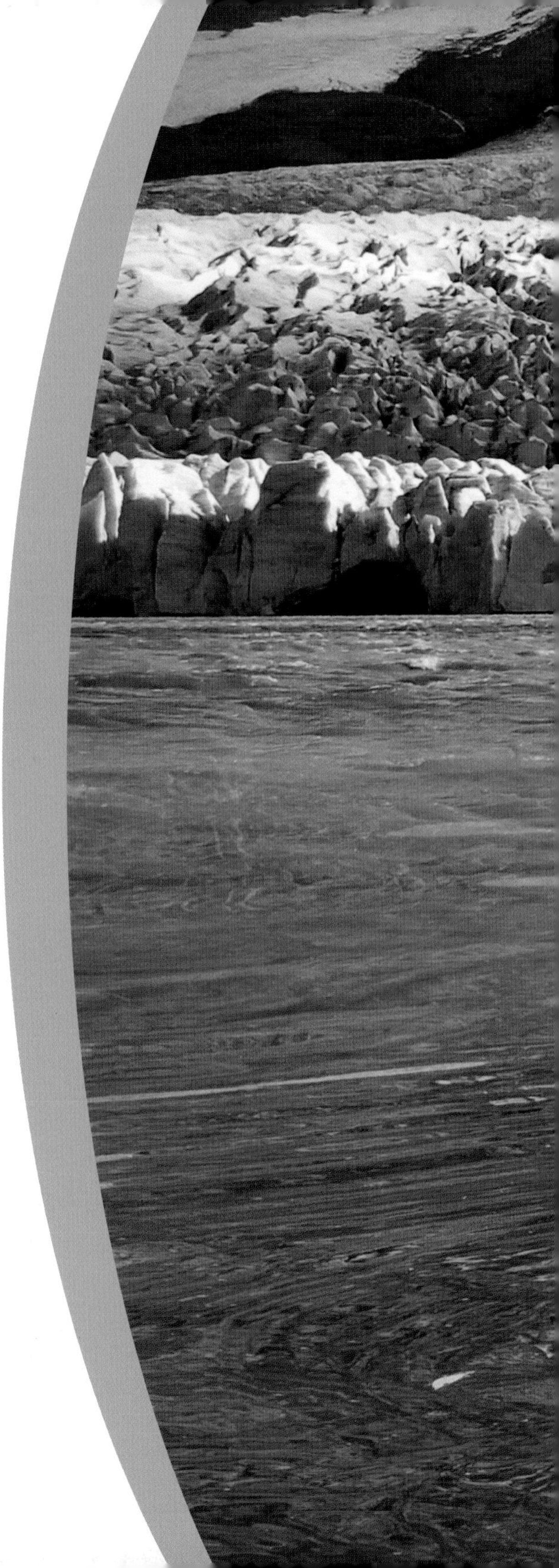

The main threat to polar bears is habitat loss. Longer, warmer seasons melt sea ice.

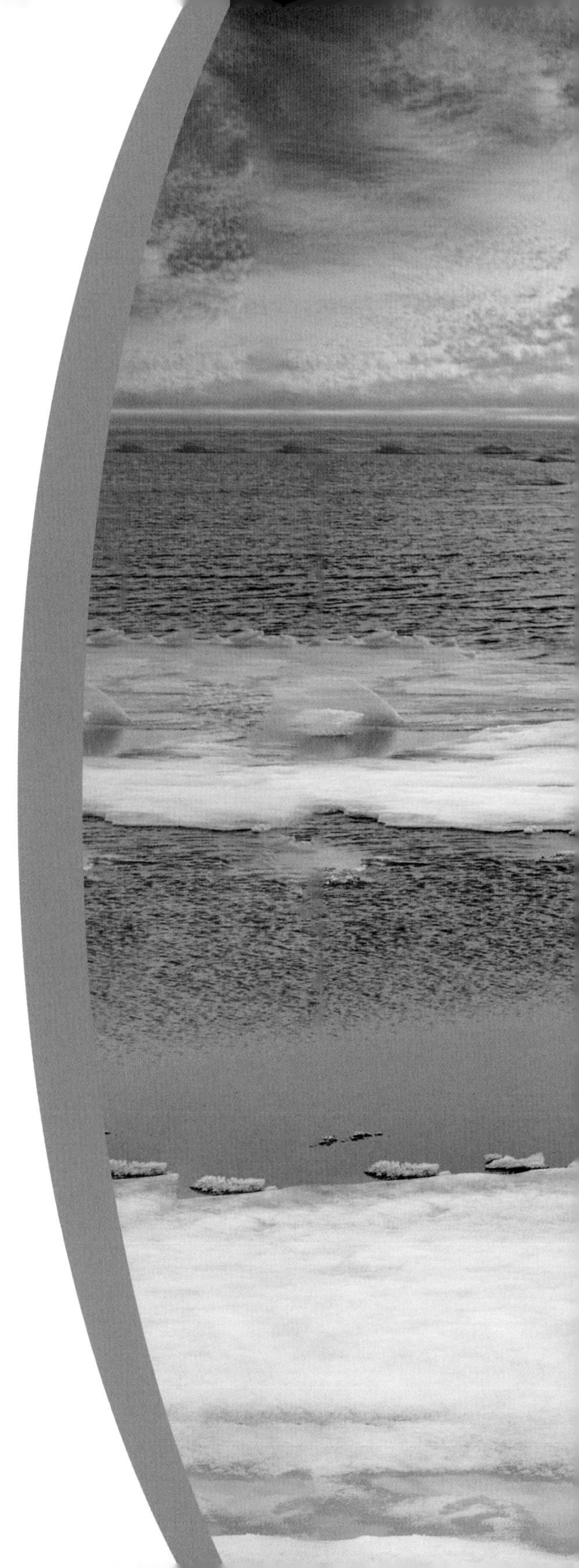

The higher temperatures are due to **climate change**. **Greenhouse gases** in the air help keep Earth warm. But too much of them is making Earth too warm.

How to Help

Fossil fuels are a part of the problem. Everyone can do a little to help a lot! Using electricity burns fossil fuels. Turn off the lights when you leave a room to help save.

Bike or walk to places near you. This saves gas. Use reusable bags instead of plastic or paper. Less **pollution** and saving trees helps polar bears and the Earth!

Polar Bears Overview

- Status: **Vulnerable**
- Population: 26,000
- Habitat: Arctic tundra and sea ice
- Greatest Threats: poaching, habitat loss, and **pollution**

Glossary

chemical – a substance that has been prepared artificially.

climate change – the increase in global average temperatures.

endangered – in danger of becoming extinct.

fossil fuel – a natural fuel such as coal or gas, formed in the geological past from the remains of living organisms.

greenhouse gas – a gas, such as carbon dioxide, that contributes to climate change if too much is given off.

pollution – poisons, wastes, or other materials that can pollute.

vulnerable – a species that is likely to become endangered unless the circumstances that are threatening its survival and reproduction improve.

Index

Visit abdokids.com and use this code to access crafts, games, videos, and more!